THE ENTERER OF THE THRESHOLD

ORDO ASTRI

THE
ENTERER
OF THE
THRESHOLD

Oliver St. John
The Enterer of the Threshold
© Oliver St. John 2016

ISBN 978-1-78808-726-1

Cover design and graphics © Oliver St. John 2016

The backcover Illustration of Horus is based on an original drawing by Jeff Dahl, wickimedia commons

ORDO ASTRI IMPRIMATUR
www.ordoastri.org

In ceremonial, the drawing of a circle is the key to all. It must be a true magical vortex—raising about the sphere of the mind an absolute barrier to all extraneous impressions—thus enabling perfect spontaneity.

CONTENTS

The Three Holy Vows

Let the student of Theurgical Arts practice and understand the Three Holy Vows of the sages of old. So there should be no mistake we set them down here in language plain and bold:

1. *Obedience* means accepting to be directed in one's work. Without this acceptance there can be no true relationship between the aspirant and the Order to which he or she aspires. Indeed, unless Obedience is practised and understood then there can be no aspiration, only vain hope—or worse.

2. *Poverty* means stripping away non-essentials and being receptive to the Hermetic Light. This automatically implies that one must liberate the self from any preconceptions regarding the latter.

3. *Chastity* means accepting to be committed to a particular method and discipline and remaining faithful to that commitment.

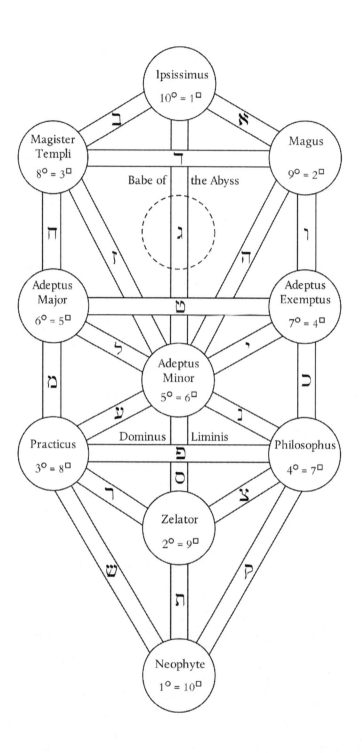

Introduction to the Order of the Star

A true magical Order will not be found on the Internet. It will not be found in books, although books are an excellent place to start. It will not be found even by meeting the persons who are members of such an Order, or who claim to represent it. Initiation does not reside in any exoteric organisation. It is discovered, and resides, within the heart and soul of the Initiate. This forms part of the gradual unfolding of the central experience of the Initiate, the Knowledge and Conversation of the Holy Guardian Angel.

The Order of the O∴ A∴ is a magical and mystical system of initiatory grades or degrees that assist the person to understand and realise Thelema as their own unique magical and spiritual path. The O∴ A∴ is not a religion, for our aim is Gnosis or Illumination, not belief. As a Thelemic Order, the general aim is for each to discover their True Will, which is the direct expression or true nature of the Self.

The aim and purpose of Ordo Astri is identical to that of the Great Work, which is to assist men and women in the obtaining of Illumination. Ordo Astri, the Order of the Star, is an Outer Order for an Invisible Collegium, presided over by Illuminated Souls, as according to tradition. These use symbols to communicate with human intelligence, such as the Egyptian Eye of Horus and Ankh of Life.

It is the aim of magick to contact the luminous Intelligences that mediate the numinous source of all, beyond all symbols and symbolism. A contacted magical Order is able to assist with this through providing various means. Ordo Astri itself is one such means, for example. It should at the same time be understood that no magical system, or the results gained, is an end in itself but that all magical systems are there to help the person reach beyond all systems.

The Light and Dark Face of the Angel

Horus is the universal symbol or type of the Holy Guardian Angel. Like all Egyptian gods, Horus is polymorphic and thus able to assume many forms such as Hoor-Apep, Heru-ra-ha and Hormaku.

The Great Work is to realise the True Self through the Knowledge and Conversation of the Holy Guardian Angel, and to help others accomplish the same. In our magical system, based on the Hermetic Tree of Life, there are three critical points in the journey of the Initiate, which are marked by the three veils of the Tree of Life. At each of these an adversary may be encountered as a force whose strength appears to match that of the aspirant, if not to actually exceed it.

The Dweller on the Threshold is first encountered before the person even sets a foot firmly on the path. This is the first spiritual crossroads, as the person considers making a firm commitment to the Great Work. They are greatly hindered by their lack of knowledge and experience. No sooner do they even consider the step, perhaps making tenuous contact with the O∴ A∴, than a tumultuous multitude appears, shouting and screaming at them to turn back.

The rebellion may manifest in the voices and actions of other people, or the circumstances of the person's life, but the real source is the undisciplined and disorganised state of the mind and soul of the candidate. It may also be that the person does not, in reality, wish to know any truth. In that case, they will soon end their association with the O∴ A∴.

The second critical point is in the attainment of the Knowledge and Conversation of the Holy Guardian Angel. Even while the aspirant is preparing their Oath and meditating on the shining one or *augoedes*, the Four Evil Princes of the World are stirring, for they seek ever to undo the magician and thwart his or her true purpose.

The third critical point is called the crossing of the Abyss, which is required before a person becomes a Master of the Temple. Crossing the Abyss requires encountering, entirely alone and without help, a force that seems to be utterly opposed to the further progress of the aspirant. Furthermore, it requires the aspirant to become 'self-slain', which is to say they must achieve the annihilation of their ego, and yet retain their sanity. Only thus may the nature of the self, and that which is called divine (*Theos*), be fully and truly realised, without the obfuscation of ego identification.

There follows a plan of the degree system and structure of the Order, which is outwardly identical to that postulated for the Order of the A∴ A∴ by Aleister Crowley in *The Equinox*, "One Star in Sight". However, please note that while *Thelema* is our basis, the O∴ A∴ does not serve as a vehicle for the rites, ceremonies or practices of Aleister Crowley or of the O. T. O.

THIRD ORDER OF THE SILVER STAR OR A∴ A∴

Ipsissimus	$10° = 1^{\square}$	Degree
Magus	$9° = 2^{\square}$	Degree
Magister Templi	$8° = 3^{\square}$	Degree

SECOND ORDER OF THE ROSY CROSS

(Babe of the Abyss is the link between 2nd and 3rd Orders)

Adeptus Exemptus	$7° = 4^{\square}$	Degree
Adeptus Major	$6° = 5^{\square}$	Degree
Adeptus Minor	$5° = 6^{\square}$	Degree

FIRST ORDER OF THE GOLDEN DAWN

(Dominus Liminis is the link between the 1st and 2nd Orders)

Philosophus	$4° = 7^{\square}$	Degree
Practicus	$3° = 8^{\square}$	Degree
Zelator	$2° = 9^{\square}$	Degree
Neophyte	$1° = 10^{\square}$	Degree

($0° = 0^{\square}$ is the passage from the Outer Darkness)

The Order of the Golden Dawn

The Egyptian Book of the Law, Liber AL vel Legis, must be read and studied from the outset, preferably before making contact with the O∴ A∴. Generally speaking, the three chapters apply to the path of Initiation in reverse: the third chapter applies to the Outer Order or Golden Dawn, the second chapter applies to the Inner Order of the Rosy Cross, and the first chapter applies to the Invisible Order of the Silver Star. The principal work of the Probationer is to discover the secret nature of their self. To this end, they will agree to perform various tasks, all the while keeping a magical diary Record of their work. Traditionally, it is said they must seek to obtain a measure of control over the nature and powers of their own being. The magical power or vision that marks the true admission to the grade of Neophyte is that of the *Holy Guardian Angel, or of Adonai.*

The rest of the degrees in the Golden Dawn are really a continuation and development of this seeking out of the secret nature of the self, and discovering the True Will. The first four degrees, Neophyte, Zelator, Practicus and Philosophus, are elemental degrees, corresponding to Earth, Air, Water and Fire, and the four faces of the Sphinx of Nature. Malkuth symbolises the Universe, as the summation of the whole Tree of Life. The other three have planetary correspondences. Yesod (Zelator) is the sphere of the Moon, Hod (Practicus) is the sphere of Mercury, and Netzach (Philosophus) is the sphere of Venus.

The Dominus Liminis ("Lord of the Threshold") is the link or passage between the 1st and 2nd Orders—it should all the while be noted that there is in reality but one Order that has three divisions for the sake of classification. The Dominus Liminis grade has no sephirotic correspondence but is theoretically located on the crossroads of the 25th and 27th paths. Elementally, the Dominus Liminis grade is Spirit as the equilibration of the four elements below. Thus, as these elements have their correspondence in the man and woman, each must seek ways to achieve this equilibrium in themselves. Traditionally, the Dominus Liminis takes an Oath in which they pledge to "obtain control of the aspirations of my self". In this grade the person should perfect their knowledge and practice of all the rituals and other methods of the Outer Order of the Golden Dawn. The magical power or vision marking true admission to the Second Order is *the vision of the harmony of all things.* This is conveyed by the Holy Guardian Angel.

The Order of the Rosy Cross

The Adeptus Minor grade ("Younger Magician") refers to Tiphereth, the sixth sephira on the Qabalistic Tree of Life, and the Sun of our solar system. At this stage of the journey the aspirant must become a mystic in the true sense of the word, for the Knowledge and Conversation of the Holy Guardian Angel is a mystical experience. The Adeptus Minor has this as their sole task to do and to achieve. The Adeptus Minor truly becomes a member of the Inner Order of the Rosy Cross when they attain the Knowledge and Conversation of the Holy Guardian Angel. They then realise themselves as an "Adeptus Within" (i.e., Within the Sanctuary).

The Adeptus Major ("Senior Magician" or "Master of Magick") refers to Geburah, the fifth sephira on the Qabalistic Tree of Life. This is the chakra of Mars. Spiritually, it corresponds to Death and so the symbolism of Initiation is the Vault or Sarcophagus. The task of the Adeptus Major is to express their True Will and no other—which is to say, the Will of the Holy Guardian Angel, not their personal self. The Adeptus Major obtains a general mastery of magick, including that which is called *Jnanamudra* in our system.

The Adeptus Exemptus ("Released") grade refers to Chesed, the fourth sephira on the Qabalistic Tree of Life. This is the chakra of Jupiter. Spiritually, this is the New Life that follows the ritual Death of the Adeptus Major. The task of the Adeptus Exemptus is to become emancipated from the bondage of reason, and to lead a pure, devoted life. This is to prepare them for the critical confrontation with the crossing of the Abyss.

The Babe of the Abyss is the link or passage between the Second and Third Orders, and has no sephirotic correspondence or paths but the non-sephira, Da'ath, the sphere of Knowledge and Abyss of the Tree of Life. Da'ath is the (false) crown of Reason, the Qabalistic Ruach. It is necessary to take the Oath of the Abyss to transcend this, the ultimate Dweller on the Threshold, and truly partake of the spiritual Neschemah or divine Intuition (Binah, the summation of the supernals). In poetic terms, borrowed from Aleister Crowley's *Vision and the Voice*, it is to become Nemo (Nameless or No-one) in the City of the Pyramids under the Night of Pan.

The Order of the Silver Star or A∴ A∴

The Magister Templi grade ("Master of the Temple") refers to Binah, the third sephira on the Qabalistic Tree of Life. This is the chakra of Saturn. The Magister Templi must take the Oath of the Abyss, which is "to interpret every phenomenon as a particular dealing of God with my Soul". The Magister Templi must become the complete mystic, an adept of impersonal love (*Agape*); they must perfect their Understanding of the Universe, and achieve *Mahamudra*.

The Magus grade ("Wizard") refers to Chokmah, the second sephira on the Qabalistic Tree of Life. The traditional mundane chakra is the Zodiac (Mazloth), the starry girdle of Nuit. This grade is very particular to the True Will, since it is the source or very root of that Self. It is also the sephirotic location of the Logos or Word. The Magus must make every Act an expression of their magical Will, and must utter a Word that creates a new world system.

The Ipsissimus grade ("Own True Self") refers to Kether, the first sephira on the Qabalistic Tree of Life. The mundane chakra is the Primum Mobile, the first movement of things. The Ipsissimus must know every phenomenon as God, which is to know the Soul of the World. The Ipsissimus is Master of all modes of existence or being, attaining All in the Great Night of Pan. Upon attaining this, the Ipsissimus withdraws at once within the shell of their humanity, keeping silence forever of the fact.

A Word on the Means

All progress is by Oath and Deed. According to Aleister Crowley (*Magick*): "A real Magical Oath cannot be broken: you think it can, but it can't. This is the advantage of a real Magical Oath."

Although anyone may solemnly write their name to a magical Oath, that does not, in itself, make it 'real'. A piece of paper, after all, is just that. In the same way, a person may be admitted to membership of an Order, but that does not mean they have truly entered any sanctuary or abode in the real sense. No ritual or ceremony will confer Initiation of its own accord, and no person on earth may confer true Initiation on another. Membership of the Order, and Initiation, are sublime matters of the soul. The work begins, nonetheless, with the *Oath of Dedication* (or Probationer Oath).

The Circle of the Place

Initiation works through the formula called the Enterer of the Threshold. The Probationer must enter the pyramid of Malkuth from 'outside' to truly become a Neophyte. They must square the infinite circle of all that they are and can ever be.

The $0° = 0^\square$ is the most important grade in the Order because it lays the foundation and provides the magical link between the Outer World of Darkness and the interior world of Illuminated Souls or inner plane Adepti. It is the aim of magick to forge contacts with the latter.

The pyramid of Malkuth must first be constructed through the effort of the Probationer, then realised through contact made with the inner planes. The Probationer degree is all about the circle of the infinite—for it has no number or sephira.

There is, further, a mystery of the Ain Soph Aur, the veils of negativity that precede Kether. The thread of the Ain Soph is the means of translation between the planes in magick and mysticism; it is the magical means of the verb, the word that goes forth. This is not something that only concerns the Probationer that is awaiting full admission to the Order, for the squaring of the circle applies to every grade and every sephira of the Tree of Life.

At the very beginning there is the intellectual matter of books, study and thought, which is the work of the Student. This work continues through all grades. Next, the magical circle must be constructed by taking the Great Work from theory into practice. The Probationer must define the magical circle of the place, squaring the $0° = 0^\square$ circle of the infinite.

The Probationer must practice and understand the following tenfold formula over the course of one year, for it is the magical and spiritual means of truly attaining the Initiation of the Enterer of the Threshold.

0. The Enterer of the Threshold 0° = 0□

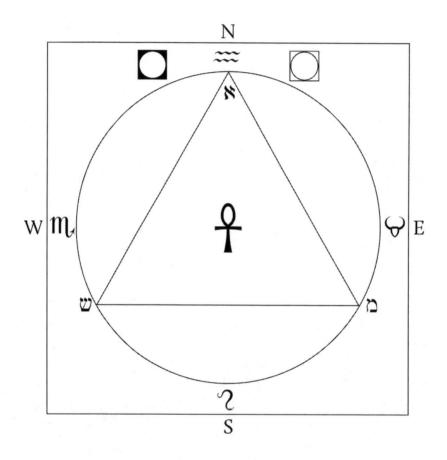

0. Intellectual thought and study.

1. The Magical Name.

2. The Oath and Task.

3. The Holy Obligation.

4. The Powers of the Sphinx.

5. The Lesser Ritual of the Pentagram.

6. The Keeping of the Record!

7. The *mudra* of Horus the Enterer and Silence.

8. Vibration of Words of Power.

9. Tantra-yoga: *Asana* and *Pranayama*.

10. The Sword and Serpent (Kether to Malkuth; Lightning Flash).

The link between the Probationer and Neophyte is the *Vision of Adonai or the Holy Guardian Angel,* which is the magical power of Malkuth. This is affirmed, whether symbolically or actually, by the O∴ A∴ ritual of Initiation called the *Phoenix.* Thus—and only thus—is the Neophyte prepared to ascend the paths of the Serpent of Wisdom from Malkuth. We can now enter into the particulars of the work.

In ceremonial, the drawing of a circle is the key to all. It must be a true magical vortex—raising about the sphere of the mind an absolute barrier to all extraneous impressions—thus enabling perfect spontaneity.[1]

The circumambulations about the circle begin with seated *asana* and *pranayama,* the circulation of the breath. All ceremonial circumambulation is an outward projection of the circulation of the breath in yoga, and is the arising of light in darkness.

---

[1] Paraphrased from Golden Dawn Flying Roll lecture XXVII.

The Exordium

The Golden Dawn Exordium is the Enterer of the Threshold preliminary to the Initiation of a Neophyte. Reflect on the meaning of this, for it is the beginning and the end, the Alpha and Omega. The Exordium is needed before anything can be created whatsoever. The correct formulation of the magical circle is given here:

Clear the mind of all extraneous thoughts.

Conceive a circle of light.

See yourself as standing on the edge of it.

Triangulate the circle (see diagram, *supra*).

Step forward so you are standing in the centre of the base line of the triangle, facing the angle in the North.

Make the mudra of the Enterer towards the North.

Make the mudra of Silence.

Realise a tetrahedronal pyramid with the apex vertically above.

(It appears spontaneously, Io!)

Withdraw the projection.

In doing this, you have symbolically—and, if you are adept, enacted in reality—the Exordium. All circumambulations and movement in the temple is widdershins in our scheme. However, when you perform the Lesser Ritual of the Pentagram, the direction of invoking the quarters is made deosil, even while the magician paces (or turns) widdershins. This is vital, for the dual Hermetic current is invoked simultaneously, Sol and Luna, Ida and Pingala, Isis and Nephthys. Behold—the living manifestation of the Caduceus of Mercury!

The General Exordium

The Speech in the Silence:
The Words against the Son of Night.
The Voice of Thoth before the Universe
In the presence of the Eternal Gods.
The Formulas of Knowledge:
The Wisdom of Breath;
The Radix of Vibration;
The Shaking of the Invisible;
The Rolling Asunder of the Darkness;
The Becoming Visible of Matter;
The Piercing of the Coils of the Stooping Dragon;
The Breaking forth of the Light.
All these are in the Knowledge of Tho-oth.

The Particular Exordium

At the Ending of the Night at the Limits of the Light
Tho-oth stood before the Unborn Ones of Time.
Then was formulated the Universe;
Then came forth the Gods thereof;
The Aeons of the Bornless Beyond.
Then was the Voice vibrated;
Then was the Name declared;
At the Threshold of the Entrance
Between the Universe and the Infinite;
In the Sign of the Enterer, stood Tho-oth
As before him were the Aeons proclaimed.
In Breath did he vibrate them;
In Symbols did he record them.
For betwixt the Light and the Darkness did he stand!

The Tree of Man: the Microcosm

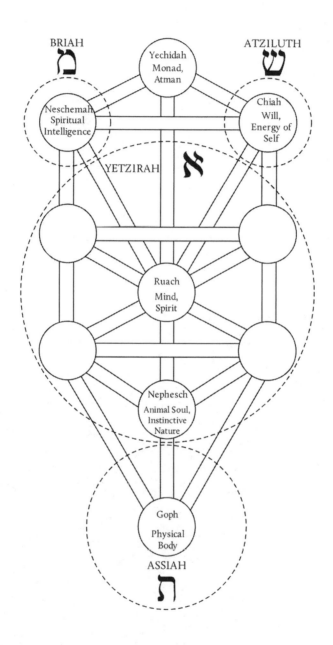

"To obtain magical power, one must strengthen the will. Let there be no confusion between will and desire. You cannot will too strongly, so do not attempt to will two things at once, and while willing one thing do not desire others.

Example: You may at times have passed a person in the street, and as soon as passed may have felt some attraction, and the will to see him again; turning round (you) may have found that he also turned to you. The will, although untrained, may have alone done this. But if you, untrained, walk out again, and decide to make the experiment of willing that he who passes you shall turn round, and try it, you will fail. Because the desire of gratifying your curiosity has weakened the force of your will."

G. H. Frater N. O. M. (Dr. W. W. Westcott)

The Tree of Life is studied and practiced as both Macrocosm and Microcosm. In the Golden Dawn or Outer Order, the work is mostly concerned with the Microcosm. The study of the greater universe, the Macrocosm, generally comes later. Nonetheless, the study of the Tree of Life in the Microcosm is not without its pitfalls. We are naturally inclined to be self reflective and self absorbed; too much of this causes the principle of the reasoning centre of consciousness, Tiphereth, to become involved with the automatic part of the self, the Nephesch. In Hermeticism, this natural tendency is actively countered by studying, meditating and working with the universal symbolism—applied to the Microcosm.

For all practical purposes, the *astrosome* or sphere of sensation is understood to be an energetic subtle or non-material (astral) body surrounding the physical body. The Astral Light is impressionable and volatile; the *astrosome*, composed of the same substance, receives the impressions made upon it by thought. As soon as the consciousness of the aspirant rises above Malkuth (as physical body), along the path of the Tav to Yesod, there is an encounter with the crosscurrents or reflections of the Astral Light. The *astrosome* has reflected the material body since birth, and consciousness has followed suit, creating a magical mirror of the self, composed from impressions. These are, as often occurs in dream, confused and misleading images.

For these reasons, discrimination is traditionally the virtue of Malkuth, while inertia (and with it, indiscipline) is the corresponding vice. The learning (and *application*) of the magical correspondences is one way we deal with this. Neophytes are urged to study the complex "Z" ceremonial formula of the Magick of Light of the Golden Dawn, for example, and to study and most of all, *practice*, the dynamic form of this presented in our *Liber CMXXX (Phoenix)*.

On the Tree of Life in the Microcosm, the *Yechidah* is the divine in man, Kether. The *Chiah* is the beginning of the Self in Chokmah. The *Neschemah* is the higher intuition located in Binah, and the *Ruach* is the human consciousness and will that is seated in Tiphereth—the ruler of the physical body. The *Nephesch* located in Yesod is the automatic consciousness, concerned with the passions, desires and needs. As it is automatic, it is "moving of itself" and cannot be said to have a will really. The human will (that *should* be seated in Tiphereth) is naturally attracted towards contemplation and union with this automatic consciousness. When that occurs, the human consciousness leaves its true place and descends to the level of the automatic consciousness.

It is a natural (and unfortunate) tendency then, in all of us, to be ruled not from the heart of Tiphereth, but from the automatic consciousness or *Nephesch*. The consciousness has abnegated the throne of will in Tiphereth, and has descended to Yesod, so that in fact it becomes 'automatic'. The person is then compelled increasingly by habitual tendencies, and is made the subject of them. This is the truer meaning of the so-called fall of Adam, or stooping down of Eve said to have brought disorder to the Tree of Life.

The automatic consciousness, when situated rightly, is in Yesod, the sphere of the Nephesch, "which attracts the material atoms". The throne of the spiritual consciousness is Da'ath. According to MacGregor Mathers, in his lecture, *The Constitution of Man*:

"You will now at once see that spiritual consciousness does not partake of the physical body but is the light which radiates. The way in which thought proceeds is by radiation; that is to say, its rays are thrown vibrating through this sphere of Astral Light."

Mathers goes on to describe "mistaken clairvoyance" as a "selfishness of the thought plane". Here, consciousness receives the reflections that have been shaped and modified by the person themselves. For example, dwelling on one's own nature with the idea of reforming and making oneself better *contracts* the consciousness and point of view—thus engendering selfishness. In like fashion, excessive asceticism becomes evil, for it tends to support notions of being better than other persons. The magician must find ways to escape these pitfalls, and find ways to climb out of them if an error is made:

"Therefore to the student that is studying clairvoyance, it is particularly advisable that he should rather repress that form of it which tends in his own direction, for fear of encouraging that spiritual selfishness which is so subtle as to escape the attention until it is too late. If he continues along this path his errors will increase, and he will arrive at a period of depression. From this will arise a series of miserable feelings which might have been checked in the beginning."

Mathers illustrates this with an example of someone in whom the influence of fiery Mars is very dominant. When this person attempts to skry, they are fairly good if the object is fire, or is of the nature of fire. The correspondence colour of fire is red, and red is what they see. However, when they regard the water element, whose correspondence is blue, what they see is violet. They have mixed into it that fiery portion of their self, and so they are unable to clearly perceive the pure element. Thus, we adulterate our perceptions through the habit of self-interest.

Mathers concludes the lecture by pointing out that the sin of the *Nephesch* or automatic consciousness is what is commonly thought of as vice. The sin of human reasoning consciousness is that of the intellectual man. The sin of spiritual consciousness is on the psychic plane. There is no vice or error, however, in the divine consciousness as posited in Kether. For that reason, it is always the task of the magician to invoke the Crown, the highest. The whole work of the Golden Dawn in the Outer is summed up in the symbol of the white triangle surmounted by the red cross. The divine consciousness, symbolised by the white triangle of the supernal sephiroth, is brought down through the self-sacrifice of Tiphereth, as symbolised by the red cross, to unite with and so rescue the lower elemental self or natural soul.

The Intelligence of Luminosity

The glyph of Venus, the lady of Love, uniquely embraces the whole Tree of Life. The title of the 14th path of Venus or Daleth, the door of the Mysteries, is the *Luminous Intelligence*, named thus because it is illuminated by Chokmah, Wisdom. Light is transmitted along the 14th path to be veiled in the form or containment of Binah. The illumination of the 14th path is the equivalent of *jnanamudra* and *mahamudra* in the Tantras; the practitioner does not cleave to the perception of phenomena (i.e., does not attach personal identity), realising clearly that all phenomena are essentially of the nature of emptiness, and that the appearance of things is merely a trick of the senses.

The Hebrew word for "illumination, luminous or shining", used to form the title of the path of Venus, is MAIR (מאיר). The root of this word is AUR (אור), "light", which can mean the light of a lamp, or the light of day, though it has a special occult significance where it refers to spirit-light, the channel by which consciousness awareness can move upwards and downwards on the planes via the middle pillar of equilibrium.

The occult meaning of AUR, the magical light, is best conveyed through the ancient Egyptian root of the word—which is spelled exactly the same when transliterated from hieroglyphics. The Egyptian AUR has many variant meanings, depending on how it is spelled and pronounced. Among these are:

To conceive

A stream or river

Radiation

Brilliance

Light

The phonetic hieroglyphs are the flowering reed and the fledgling. The whole mystery of parthenogenesis—the conception of a magical child without paternal or physical intervention—is explained by the Egyptian AUR. This is the real occult secret and the potency behind the Magick of Light or "Z" formula that begins and ends with the Enterer of the Threshold, for it is that which the alchemists figured as AZOTH.

The Occult Science

Since it is our wish to get away as far as possible from reductionism and psychologisation of the mysteries, we use the traditional term *Occult Science* to describe the subject of our interest. Direct knowledge or Gnosis has always been suppressed by religious authorities, along with the traditional occult practices that may lead to it, especially divination and prophecy, because it always contradicts scriptural laws and prohibitions.

The Occult Science is not the same thing at all as conventional science, and will never be proved or understood by the methods of the latter. With material science, the general idea is that something is "proved" by repeated experiments with control conditions. While magick involves repeated experiments, as metaphorically demonstrated in a host of anonymously written alchemical treatises, the "proving" is not the same. The immortal stone cannot be weighed or measured. According to material science, the human soul does not exist beyond the realm of imagining, for likewise it cannot be weighed or measured.

The proving of magick is not that of intellectual persuasion, but is akin to the proving of bread when the action of yeast causes it to rise. For this reason, bread became a widely used metaphor for the 'substance' of the soul, and wine a metaphor for the spirit. Soul and spirit are unknown to material science, for that which is not material in its basis cannot be proven by material experiments or actions; so it shall always be—never the twain shall meet. The Christian mystic Meister Ekhart put this aptly when luminously commenting on "no man can serve two masters", from the book of Matthew, 6: 24:[2]

The two eyes of the soul of man cannot both perform their work at once: but if the soul shall see with the right eye into eternity, then the left eye must close itself and refrain from working, and be as though it were dead. For if the left eye be fulfilling its office toward outward things, that is holding converse with time and the creatures; then must the right eye be hindered in its working; that is, in its contemplation. Therefore, whosoever will have the one must let the other go; for 'no man can serve two masters.'

---

[2] From *Theologia Germanica*, Meister Ekhart.

The method called the Keeping of the Record is central to the Occult Science. The Record is established in primary magical training, comprising the core discipline. It is also a sharp sword that disposes of would-be candidates that imagine their superficial interest in the mysteries to be something more. Magick is Hermes-Mercury, and the Egyptian Thoth is after all the *Logos*, the god of scribes and of writing. With our 'scientific' method of keeping the magical diary Record, the intention is to build a bridge between the deeper levels of consciousness accessed through theurgic practices and the ordinary waking mode of consciousness.

The ritual or meditation, if this has been effectively done, does not end with a closing or 'banishing' ritual, it goes on working in the background continuously even while we engage with mundane tasks.[3] Furthermore, the writing up of the Record is part of the ritual; failing to write the Record is to leave a work undone. When consciousness is liberated from its usual preoccupations and has penetrated beyond what Occult Science terms as the Astral plane to the Hermetic plane—something approaching though not yet wholly absorbed in the pure or Deep Mind of the Tibetan Tantras—then we have left conventional thought far behind. On returning to the usual mode of thought, subtle nuances or impressions may be 'unpacked'. What may have taken place in an immeasurable moment might fill a whole page in the journal. The technique of what to write and what to leave out has therefore to be learned over time.

In our diary Record we keep faithful observances. There are traditional factors for inclusion such as the astrological positions of the Sun and Moon, as well as the time started and the time finished. We can add to that such things as how we are feeling that day, and what the weather is like. When reviewing the Record at a later date we then have a great deal of information to help our evaluation.

---

[3] The term "banishing ritual" is unfortunate. It is better to think of a "closing ritual". When a ritual is perfectly done, nothing remains, as with a Eucharist—the work is done, accomplished. "Banishing" leads novices to adopt the wrong attitude towards elemental or nature spirits. Industrial and motorcar pollution has laid to waste woodlands and wildlife, the natural habitat for nature spirits. Where nature spirits once played, abominations and horrors now lurk, that will eventually destroy their unwitting human engineers.

At the time of writing this, the Sun and Moon are in Virgo. From that information alone I will know in future that my train of thought took place at the dark of the Moon in the sign of the Virgin, poetically the "blood of Isis". The sea will be at the highest and lowest tidal mark.

Environmental factors are far more difficult to determine than astrological factors. For example, I live on a narrow strip of land locally called "the Island", surrounded on three sides by the Celtic Sea. We Island dwellers are sensitive to whether the tide is in or out, whether it is a spring tide or a neap tide—factors determined by the lunar phases. On the other hand, the town is a popular holiday resort, so in the summer months the psychic planes are cluttered to an extent where sensitives suffer headaches and disturbing dreams or sleepless nights. A cloud of dissociated recreational *angst* descends on the place, added to increased pollution and noise from crowds, cars, motorbikes and service vehicles. Each person must therefore work out their unique environmental conditions, while bearing in mind that placing too much attention on such phenomena is a recipe for psychosis and may lead the aspirant far, far away from the Heart of the Master.

It is impossible to create a perfect model for such observances, which applies as much to the timing of a magical operation as it does to the Keeping of the Record. An astrological horoscope is a complex figure, requiring great expertise to produce a judgment. Even then, one cannot take account of every factor in an infinite universe. We have to choose our parameters and then stick to them. The so-called planetary hours—a system much abhorred by the anonymous 15th century author of *The Sacred Magic of Abramelin the Mage*—turns out to be a very useful way to time certain kinds of magical operations. Abramelin and his admirers, including MacGregor Mathers and Aleister Crowley, condemned the planetary hours system as "arbitrary" because it bears to relation to the actual positions of the planets. However, the same argument applies to any symbolic scheme, whether 'scientific' or not. The primary objection of Abramelin was that people used the tables of hours superstitiously and did not know what they were doing. If we know what we are doing and why we are doing it, then planetary hours become a powerful and practical method of organising time; it is a discipline that consecrates particular days and hours to a sevenfold symbol of the universe.

Confusion between scientism, or material science orthodoxy, and the Occult Science produces obsession with the 'wrong kind of errors'. To cite an example, there are some who vigorously argue that the Tibetan (or other) systems of sidereal and tropical astrology contain errors in calculation. There is much scholarly debate about sidereal as opposed to tropical systems. In fact, the ancient astrologers employed both systems to suit different purposes. The universe is full of infinite errors to those uninitiated in the true meaning of the way of the *Kalachakra* wheel of time. The aim of the way of *Kalachakra Tantra* is to unite with the deities, comparable to Nuit and Hadit that look *both inside and outside of time.*[4]

When we become liberated from temporal restriction on consciousness then the eye, fixed on eternity, perceives no errors or flaws in anything whatsoever. This brings us back to the Meister Ekhart comment on the book of Matthew that we cited earlier. It will be helpful to supply the whole quotation, in context, from Matthew 6: 21–24:

For where your treasure is, there will your heart be also.

The light of the body is the eye: if therefore thine eye be single, thy whole body shall be full of light. But if thine eye be evil, thy whole body shall be full of darkness.

If therefore the light that is in thee be darkness, how great is that darkness!

No man can serve two masters: for either he will hate the one, and love the other; or else he will hold to the one, and despise the other. Ye cannot serve God [*Theos*] and mammon.

A man has two eyes, one that looks onto the material world, and another that can see beyond the world of ever-changing phenomena and directly into eternity. These are entirely different modes of consciousness; one functions under what is termed "Restriction" in Liber AL vel Legis, I: 41:

The word of Sin is Restriction.

---

[4] The principal deities of the Tibetan and Hindu *Kalachakra Tantra* are Kalachakra and Kalachakri, or Ishtadevata, identical to Hadit and Nuit, Shiva and Shakti, etc.

Sin or error, literally, "missing the mark", comes about from the *contraction of consciousness*. In this state of restricted or shortened force, there can be no accounting for the "space marks", the periodic flow of *kalas* that interpenetrates and moves through and across the bounds of the temporal and the eternal. In I: 52 of the book of Nuit, the queen of space declares:

If this be not aright; if ye confound the space-marks, saying: They are one; or saying, They are many; if the ritual be not ever unto me: then expect the direful judgments of Ra Hoor Khuit!

Restriction is the ordinary condition of human consciousness, flawed and incomplete, yet bedazzled and intoxicated with the apparent power of the reasoning intellect. What we see is what we *are*, no more and no less. The eye fixed on the eternal is clear of karmic 'errors', for it is contained within the knowledge that there is no causality in reality, that every phenomenon arises spontaneously upon the face of the void-absolute, having no essential root or substance from its own side. There are no causes and no effects.

What then, can we make of the following definition of magick, as formulated by Aleister Crowley?

Magick is the Science and Art of causing Change to occur in conformity with Will.

Firstly, it has to be said that this is probably the best rationalisation of magick that anyone has attempted. Dion Fortune (Violet Firth) thought to modify this, so that it read, "changes in consciousness". Far from being an improvement, this has made matters even worse. While Crowley's definition inevitably opens the way to humanistic determinism—an argument that has gone on for millennia and that can never be proven either way—Dion Fortune's amendment has been seized on and fully exploited by psychological reductionists. Perhaps that is a legacy, the little mote of dust not dissolved in the cucurbit, from Aleister Crowley's intention when writing the book *Magick* to appeal to "men of science".

What is important is whether magick works or does not work, and that is what everyone must discover for their self. It is by the way that as soon as the answer to that question is known, it ceases to have any importance.

The psychological or reductionist school of magick is incapable, in spite of its claims, of producing alchemical gold. It can only succeed as a force of anti-Initiation since it posits that the human mind may produce a miracle through a 'process' or rearrangement of its own elements, the *prima materia*. On the contrary, 'gold' is extracted from the *prima materia*, that which obscures it.

The Angel, the Devil and the Master of Duality

In Chapter IV of *The Egyptian Revival*, Frater Achad (Charles Stansfeld Jones) provides the following insight into the dual nature of the Holy Guardian Angel:

We have seen in tracing out the Traditions that there have been two Wills at work, the Divine and the Personal, and that through the Ages these have appeared in conflict. One is the Bright Star or Pentagram of Unconquered Will, the other the Dark Star of the Reversed Pentagram. These two Stars are symbolised by the hands of Man, or the Magician, one raised to Heaven in the Sign of Solvé, the other directed downwards in the Sign of Coagula. When united they form a Ten-fold Star, just as the hand of the man who has fallen may be grasped by the one who Raises him in the Grip of the Lion, which exactly symbolises this uniting of the Rising and Setting Sun, or the Twins Sut-Har. For the Two Wills are Harmonised in Tiphereth. But when we consider Malkuth, it is a question of Raising the Fallen Daughter, the Animal Soul, or matter, to the Throne of the Mother, Understanding ... The Union of the two Stars as a Ten-fold Star in Malkuth is the Work before us ... as promised by the Rainbow of the old order.

This one idea alone provides us with an opportunity to gain an overview of the whole path of Initiation. From the tenfold union of the upright and averse pentagrams comes forth the elevenfold star, which is the key to magical Initiation.

According to Aleister Crowley, the number 11 is "The general number of magick, or energy tending to change".[5] The number 11 is also that of Nuit, according to the Egyptian Book of the Law, Liber AL vel Legis, I: 60:

---

[5] Aleister Crowley, *Liber 777 & other Qabalistic writings*.

My number is 11, as are all their numbers who are of us.[6]

Da'ath, Knowledge, is the eleventh sephira—really a *non-sephira*. To understand the significance of the elevenfold star of Thelemic Initiation, we need to examine the importance of Malkuth the Kingdom in the whole scheme of things.

Building the Pyramid

The magical formula of the Neophyte may apply to each of the three Orders of the Golden Dawn, Rosy Cross and Silver Star. The Golden Dawn "Z" Formula expresses the Magick of Light, the Sword (descending current) and Serpent (ascending current). The Sword and Serpent is also the key symbolism of the grade of $5° = 6^\square$, Adeptus Minor. There is no difference between Adonai, as the ascending Serpent Power within the Initiate, and Typhon or Apophis.

The ritual chamber of Malkuth may be conceived as a womb and tomb for Initiation. The four walls beyond the magick circle are the four classical elements, the faces of the Sphinx of Nature and cardinal directions. In our dynamic version of the Golden Dawn Neophyte "Z" ritual, the *Phoenix*, the circle is triangulated by two officers wearing the masks of Isis (Hegemon) and Horus (Hiereus), plus a third 'invisible station' of Thoth as the Word or Logos, the reconciler of the dual forces. Once the circle is triangulated in this way, the vertical projection from the centre evokes the apex of the pyramid above. This comes about spontaneously in the same way that the six-fold hexagram appears above and below the magician when four pentagrams are placed around the circle in the Lesser Ritual of the Pentagram. The inner aspect of Malkuth is defined here by a *tetrahedronal* pyramid, whose apex is, figuratively speaking, Iacchus or the Holy Guardian Angel. The tetrahedron is not only a symbol corresponding to the 31st path of *The Aeon XX*, but is also a symbol of Da'ath, the eleventh sephira that is yet not a sephira as such. It is the key to magical transmutation.

---

[6] Note that $\sum (1–11) = 66$, the Mystic Number of Da'ath and of the Qliphoth, therefore the Great Work of the transmutation of the Qliphoth. The number 66 is also that of "trial or test, proving", and "us". The word "us" occurs four times in Liber AL vel Legis: I: 60, II: 19 (twice) and II: 20. Furthermore, the number 66 is that of the secret garden of Nu (GNVZ).

Isis, or the Hegemon in the Neophyte ceremony, is the aspect of the Holy Guardian Angel that speaks kind words on behalf of the soul. Horus, or the Hiereus, is the Darkness of the Soul that must be overcome by the Candidate. These may be understood as dual aspects of the Holy Guardian Angel. The third aspect is symbolised by the "invisible station" of Thoth behind the two pillars in the Hall of Double Maat. Thoth, or Tahuti, stands in the sign of the Enterer until the moment that the Candidate swears the oath at the altar—for one must speak true words in the presence of the Gods. Thoth then draws back in the sign of Silence.

Attaining the Summit: Mithras, the Aeon of Aeons

Aleister Crowley made a valuable contribution to the Occult Science when he organised the "magical powers", trances or visions, in his tables of correspondences in 777. One thing distinguishing this so-called system of attainment from any other spiritual and magical path is that the Qabalah provides a map of consciousness. By combining Patanjali's *Eight Limbs of Yoga*, and his own elucidation of the yogic states from *dharana* through *dhyana* to *samadhi* and beyond, along with the Rosicrucian grade system and the entire armorium of magical practices, Aleister Crowley provided us with a very powerful means of Initiation into magick and mysticism. Here, magick and mysticism are not to be regarded as separate. Rather, magick is the means by which we may know that which the great sages of old knew, whether they could speak of it or not.

In the table following we have made additions to the non-sephirotic grades of Babe of the Abyss and Dominus Liminis; the rest are taken verbatim from 777. The 'trances' are abstruse, yet their practical usefulness is great to the magician with serious intent. Unless the *Vision of Adonai* is obtained by the Neophyte, there can be no meaning to any of the grades that follow. Unless the *Vision of Beauty Triumphant* is a natural consequence of the development of yogic concentration towards prolonged *dhyana*, then it is no more than ordinary self-delusion. We include only the sephiroth that relate to the grades, not the paths or intelligences that divine them.

25

$10° = 1^\square$	Ipsissimus	*Union with God*
$9° = 2^\square$	Magus	*Vision of God (face to face)*
$8° = 3^\square$	Magister Templi	*Vision of Sorrow & Trance of Wonder*
---	Babe of the Abyss	*Dissolution & Genesis*
$7° = 4^\square$	Adeptus Exemptus	*Vision of Love*
$6° = 5^\square$	Adeptus Major	*Vision of Power*
$5° = 6^\square$	Adeptus Minor	*Mysteries of the Crucifixion & Vision of Harmony*
---	Dominus Liminis	*Veil of Paroketh*
$4° = 7^\square$	Philosophus	*Vision of Beauty Triumphant*
$3° = 8^\square$	Practicus	*Vision of Splendour (Ezekiel)*
$2° = 9^\square$	Zelator	*Vision of the Machinery of the Universe*
$1° = 10^\square$	Neophyte	*Vision of the Holy Guardian Angel or of Adonai*

As was traditional in the Eastern Tantras, the magical powers, so-called, must be renounced as soon as gained. The practical importance of this renunciation of the powers will be made clearer if we look at the case of the Adeptus Major, a relatively lofty grade in any magical Order. This grade corresponds to Geburah or Mars on the Tree of Life, a fiery and destructive force. A cognate Egyptian god would be Horus in the form of Menthu or Typhon—the burning heat of the sun in unmitigated strength. Geburah is very close to the Veil of the Abyss, in fact it is one of the four sephiroth that form the 'womb of the Abyss' surrounding the non-sephira Da'ath.

When ascending the chakras of the Tree of Life, a descent is made simultaneously into the depths of the Tree of Knowledge or Death, the higher the branches the deeper the roots. Nonetheless, due to some quirk of human nature it helps us get on with an extremely difficult and arduous undertaking if we employ a few conventional myths along the way, such as "attainment", as though we were climbing a summit—*as though we were actually going somewhere.*

This 'going forth' requires tremendous accumulated energy.[7] However, as we plunge onward through the Trees of Eternity to the borders of the abysmal outermost, there is a complete reversal of magical polarity. Whereas the motion of the sephiroth below Da'ath is *centrifugal*—which gives rise to 'consciousness expansion'—the motion of Da'ath is *centripetal*. This powerful force sucks or draws the adept inexorably inward. That same force amounts to the annihilation of the human ego. Returning to our Adeptus Major, he or she has to obtain the *Vision of Power*. For that reason, it is set down in the Task of the grade that the Adeptus must use all powers to serve the Ideal of the Order. The principle of selflessness is paramount here. The *Vision of Love* in the grade that follows cannot be realised unless the *Vision of Power* is understood and (therefore) thoroughly renounced. Refusal to do this, resistance to the path, results in one or both of two things:

1. The person becomes a "Black Brother"

2. The person goes (actually) insane

The "Black Brother" is a term coined by Aleister Crowley to describe an adept that remains on the threshold or frontier of the Abyss for the purpose of invading and controlling the minds of others. To prevent the natural force of Da'ath from annihilating ego, the person must obtain the blood of sacrificial victims or, to put it in other terms (though equally romantic), they prey on others after the manner of a vampire.

Magick is indeed a grave business, and so we need all the help we can get if we are going to dedicate our lives and our love to a Great Work. Magick is a science, but not in the conventional sense of what that means. "Science", derived from the Latin word, *scientia,* in turn derived from *scire*, means *to know*. To know as we are known is a lesser form of the magical vision of Chokmah. Magick is also very much an art. Without art—"creative skill and imagination", as termed in the dictionary—all of this amounts to that which cannot be described in better terms than those of the fantasist H. P. Lovecraft, in *The Haunter of the Dark*:

---

[7] That energy is in itself a sacrifice that very few men and women are ever likely to make, and is one reason why such a discipline still serves an elite, especially in a technological slave culture where time is a debt that can never be paid off.

He thought of the ancient legends of Ultimate Chaos, at whose centre sprawls the blind idiot god Azathoth, Lord of All Things, encircled by his flopping horde of mindless and amorphous dancers, and lulled by the thin monotonous piping of a daemoniac flute held in nameless paws.

And here is the rub: how can we know that the *Trump of the Aeon* is not the daemoniac fluting of the blind idiot god Azathoth? And how do we know that in love's embrace it is not the "thin monotonous piping" that we hear, mistaken for the word of Israfel, or of an Holy Guardian Angel? It was a brilliant stroke of black magic to confuse the science of *knowing* with the trick of gathering data and then using technological means of rhetoric undreamed of by Aristotle to persuade mass populations that the power of reason is invincible, an absolute truth in itself.[8] All proving, other than the 'proving' of the bread that fortifies the body and the fermenting of the wine that nourishes the soul, leads us back inevitably to the primary delusion of self-identification.

In the final measure, we have abandoned rhetoric and resorted to poetry. Perhaps the last word is best left to Nuit, whose "non-atomic" voice and presence has moved every true lover since time immemorial. As it is recorded in the Egyptian Book of the Law, Liber AL vel Legis I: 3–4:

Every man and every woman is a star.

Every number is infinite; there is no difference.

---

[8] Notably television and more recently the Internet, which are together the primary instrument for the hypnotic control of minds and (therefore) bodies—an instrument all the more insidious since it persuades the person to believe that they, the individual, are in control. Aristotle put forward three tenets for the composition of rhetoric, or "persuasion": Ethos, Logos and Pathos. See *Dreaming Thelema of Kenneth Grant and H. P. Lovecraft*, Chapter VI, for a Thelemic interpretion of these, and an explanation as to how they have been corrupted in the technological age.

Hermetic and Brotherly Love

The passages that follow are extracts from Flying Roll XIII, *Hermetic and Brotherly Love*, by founder of the Hermetic Order of the Golden Dawn, S. L. MacGregor Mathers.

The natural man is a chaotic mass of contradictory forces. In the higher grades of the First Order (by presenting a perfectly balanced series of symbols to the senses), we endeavour to impress upon the imagination of the initiates, the forms under which they can obtain perfection and work in harmony with the world force.

The principles most insisted on are Secrecy and Brotherly Love. Apart entirely from the practical necessity for secrecy in our Order, it is the fact that Silence is in itself a tremendous aid in the search for Occult powers. In darkness and stillness the Archetypal forms are conceived and the forces of nature germinated. If we study the effects of calm concentration we shall find that in silence, thoughts which are above human consciousness clothe themselves with symbolism and present things to our imagination, which cannot be told in words.

On the opinions of other people

Free yourselves from your environments. Believe nothing without weighing and considering it for yourselves; what is true for one of us, may be utterly false for another. The God who will judge you at the day of reckoning is the God who is within you now; the man or woman who would lead you this way or that, will not be there then to take the responsibility off your shoulders.

On Hermetic Love:

Any love for a person as an individual is by no means a Hermetic virtue; it simply means that the personalities are harmonious; we are born under certain influences, and with certain attractions and repulsions and, just like the notes in the musical scale some of us agree, some disagree. We cannot overcome these likes and dislikes; even if we could, it would not be advisable to do so. If in Nature, a plant were to persist in growing in soil unsuited to it, neither the plant nor the soil would be benefited.

The plant would dwindle, and probably die, the soil would be impoverished to no good end ... Therefore brotherly love does not imply seeking, or remaining in the society of those to whom we have an involuntary natural repulsion.

Each individual must arrive at the consciousness of Light in his own way; and all we can do for each other is to point out that the straight and narrow path is within each of us. No man flies too high with his own wings; but if we try to force another to attempt more than his strength warrants, his inevitable fall will lie at our door.

ΘΕΛΗΜΑ
A Qabalistic Examination of the Word of the Law

0. The "word of the Law" is revealed in Liber AL vel Legis, I: 39–40:

The word of the Law is Θελημα.

Who calls us Thelemites will do no wrong, if he look but close into the word. For there are therein Three Grades, the Hermit, and the Lover, and the man of Earth. Do what thou wilt shall be the whole of the Law.

The fulfilment of the spiritual and magical Law of Thelema is declared in the Egyptian Book of the Law, Liber AL vel Legis, I: 57:

Invoke me under my stars! Love is the law, love under will.

1. The Greek word Thelema, "Will", has the Qabalistic value of 93, equal to *Agape*, which is spiritual or impersonal love. The word is frequently translated in scripture as "charity", in the archaic not the modern sense of the word. Will (*Thelema*) and Love (*Agape*) are synonymous and so perfectly equal, one with the other. As the will of Thelema is not wish or want, so the love of *Agape* is not desire for human bonding.

2. We are instructed to "look but close into the word" Thelema, for it secretes the whole path of magical Initiation. The Greek word *theletes* means, "one who wills; a wizard"—a magical practitioner. The root of the word is *thelu*, which means, "female". The word of the Law was transmitted in I: 39 of the Book by the ancient Egyptian cosmic Shakti, the Star Goddess Nuit, and yet the Thelemic True Will is often confused with the solar-masculine will of reason. The magical *consciousness current* is not concerned with the need of the human ego to make choices or decisions, to determine this or that. Thelema should not be confused with philosophical determinism—though it frequently is.

3. The first two letters, ΘΕ, are the root of *Thea*, the Goddess or divine creatrix, and *Theos*, God or deity. *Thea* also has the meaning of "a view", the window of vision and creative imagining that is symbolised in the Tarot trump *The Star XVII*. The first two letters then refer to the grade of the Hermit or devotee that follows Nuit through the starry heavens.

4. The second two letters, ΛΗ, form the root of *lema*, will, and also strength or courage. "Do what thou wilt" is not "do whatever you want"; it is to follow the course of the True Will as a star in the body of Nuit. This is a discipline that requires special courage, strength and determination. ΛΗ is also the root of Leda; in the Greek myth Zeus begat Castor and Pollux upon Leda, the polar twins of the zodiacal sign of Gemini and Tarot Atu VI *The Lovers*. ΛΗ thus signifies the grade of the Lover.

5. The last two letters, ΜΑ, are the root of *magia* or magick, *maia*, the mother of illusion, and *iama*, remedy. To transcend the illusions of the Terrestrial Plane, the Man of Earth must practice and learn the magick arts. The motivation to start a Great Work stems from a realisation that something is not right in the world. It is the plight of the fisher-king in the Graal mysteries that is 'wounded in the thigh'. The thigh is a common euphamism for the sexual and generative organs, associated with Scorpio—the crux of the whole matter of life and death. The wounded king sends his knights—his desire and imagination—out on the quest for the holy Graal. When the king is ailing, so is the whole land; the king is a symbol of the human ego in Tiphereth while the land (mother earth) is Malkuth the Kingdom, "As above, so below".

6. ΜΑ has the value of 41 and so is Qabalistically equal to *latha*, forgetfulness. The awakening of the Man of Earth, if it comes, is tenuous; how easy it is for him or her to fall back into the sleep of forgetfulness symbolised by the ancient Greeks as the waters of Lethe in Hades (hell or the underworld). Hades is hidden among the roots of the Tree in Malkuth. The Lover that has attained the Knowledge and Conversation of the Holy Guardian Angel has remembered, and has the task of constantly renewing this remembrance by making every act an Act of Will. Lethe is a reminder that even the Lover can succumb once more to the sleep of forgetfulness.

7. The outer level of teaching for the grade of the Man of Earth is the *Law*, scripture or precepts governing conduct.

8. The second or inner level of teaching for the grade of the Lover is the ability to interpret symbol and allegory in various ways that lead to deeper knowledge, for example, the use of Qabalah.

9. The third or innermost level of teaching for the grade of Hermit is the radiance of pure knowledge that is obtained when each symbol is followed back to its source with the infinite.

10. Thelema is the Tele-Ma, the talisman, *telesmata* or stellar transmission of the Mother Mu or Maat. It is revealed *and concealed* in Liber AL (*or L = 30*) vel Legis, the Book of the Law of Maat.

O∴ A∴

OATH & TASK OF A PROBATIONER 0° = 0□

Aspirants must use the correct style of address in all written communications with the Order. The letters from their Guide will show the correct style, e.g. "Care Frater" or "Cara Soror", with the tenets from the Egyptian Book of the Law, Liber AL vel Legis, inserted (accurately) at the appropriate points. Probationers are required to read carefully through the following Oath and Task, and meditate upon the meaning therein.

Probationers must practice and understand the elevenfold spiritual tenet, *Do what thou wilt shall be the whole of the Law*, and its sevenfold completion, *Love is the law, love under will*.

In doing so, it should be understood that in the outer darkness of the world, "love" and "will" are alike unto *Eros* and *Thanatos*; yet in the interior worlds of spirit and in the eternal light of wisdom, these two are known as *Agape* and *Logos*.

The Probationer must maintain a magical diary Record, which they are prepared to submit to the O∴ A∴ if and when required. Any termination of membership, whether of your own instance or that of the Order, is irrevocable.

I, _____ [ordinary name],

do hereby resolve on this _____ day of _____ Anno

_____ Sol in _____° of _____ that I shall direct the whole nature

and all the powers of my being towards the accomplishment of

the Great Work, which is: To obtain True Knowledge of that

which is by Nature hidden from the ordinary senses and reason

of Man.

May Horus crown the work, so I shall understand the work!

Witness my hand:

Frater / Soror _____

O∴ A∴

OATH & TASK OF A NEOPHYTE 1° = 10▫

Neophytes are required to read carefully through the following Oath. Having signed the form, they return a copy to the O∴ A∴, retaining the original for their own records.

Obtain a robe suitable for a Neophyte. You will be known as a Frater or Soror of the Order by your magical name and number, which is to represent your Aspiration.

The Neophyte must practise and understand the Powers of the Sphinx, and be prepared to work towards an understanding of their Initiation as it unfolds. You shall construct and consecrate the magical Pentacle, according to instruction.

A Neophyte may withdraw from the association of the O∴ A∴ by simply notifying their contact in the Order.

I, _____ [motto], do hereby resolve on this _____ day of _____ Anno _____ Sol in ____° of ____ to prosecute the Great Work, which is: To obtain control over the nature and powers of my own being. Thus and not otherwise shall I do my True Will on the earth.

Furthermore, I solemnly pledge to serve the Order faithfully, to honour its members, and to do my utmost to uphold its principles.

May Horus crown the work, and bring me to Initiation in due course!

Witness my hand:

Frater / Soror _____

O∴ A∴
OATH & TASK OF A ZELATOR 2° = 9▫

Read through this note of office and sign it, returning a copy to the O∴ A∴ The Record should show further development of the techniques of Hermetic Tantra-yoga, the wisdom of breath. You shall construct and consecrate the magical Dagger, and in every way penetrate to the heart of the Mystery of Life that is within you.

Zelators must work on the behalf of the O∴ A∴ upon their own responsibility.

Be warned that the word Zelator implies the awakening and inflaming of a certain Zeal, it will tend to take place whether or not the person realises or understands why this is so! The Zelator may withdraw at any moment from the association of the O∴ A∴ simply by notifying their immediate superior within the Order.

When the time for advancement comes, it is well to bear in mind that this is the first departure from the middle pillar of the Tree of Life, and that which is called *equilibrium*.

I, _____ [motto], do

hereby resolve on this _____ day of _____ Anno

_____ Sol in _____° of _____, that I shall apply all of my

energy to the Great Work, so that my innermost secret Self shall

be the very foundation of my existence.

May Horus crown the work, and bring me to knowledge in due course!

Witness my hand:

Frater / Soror _____

O∴ A∴
OATH & TASK OF A PRACTICUS 3° = 8□

Read through this note of office and sign it, returning a copy to the O∴ A∴ The Practicus is expected to prove their knowledge of the Qabalah. You must in every way devote your intelligence to the Great Work. For any truthful advancement in Initiation, there is a corresponding Ordeal. The solemn nature of these oaths is to give your full attention to the nature of the Great Work, which is necessarily a matter of utmost gravity.

You shall commence meditation practices aimed at consciousness expansion and the destruction of thought. Furthermore, you must show familiarity and experience with an approved method of divination, though the ultimate test of these things rests in yourself, and especially in your continued vigilance with the magical diary Record. You shall construct and consecrate the magical Cup.

Concerning the grade of Practicus, tradition teaches that Action is the Equilibrium of him that is in the House of Mercury, who is the Lord of Intelligence. Be prepared to *act* in accordance with that sacred knowledge.

Be warned that when the time comes for advancement, it shall be your *second* departure from the middle pillar of the Tree of Life, from that which is called *equilibrium*. A member of the grade of Practicus must not attempt to withdraw from association with the O∴ A∴

I, _____ [motto], do

hereby resolve on this _____ day of _____ Anno _____

Sol in ____° of ____, that I shall direct the whole of my

intelligence to the proving of the Great Work. Furthermore, I

shall act decisively in every way according to my True Will. May

Horus crown the work, and bring me to wisdom in due course!

Witness my hand:

Frater / Soror _____

O∴ A∴
OATH & TASK OF A PHILOSOPHUS 4° = 7□

Read through this note of office and sign it, returning a copy to the O∴ A∴ The Philosophus is expected to be proficient in skrying, and to strive towards union with deity.

You shall continue to practise yoga and other techniques as required, and are expected to be proficient in the technique of Rising on the Planes. You shall construct and consecrate the magical Wand.

Concerning the grade of Philosophus, tradition teaches that Philosophy is the Equilibrium of him that is in the House of Venus that is the Lady of Love.

Be mindful that you shall be expected to continuously make profound reflections upon the Path, and that you must be prepared to devote yourself utterly to the Great Work.

I, _____ [motto], do hereby resolve on this _____ day of _____ Anno _____ Sol in _____° of _____, that I shall direct the whole of my desire to the consummation of the Great Work, which is: To do my True Will and no other.

May Horus crown the work with wisdom, and bring me to illumination in due course!

Witness my hand:

Frater / Soror _____

O∴ A∴

OATH & TASK OF A DOMINUS LIMINIS

Read through this note of office and sign it, returning a copy to the O∴ A∴

The Dominus Liminis is expected to harmonise perfectly all the knowledge they have acquired thus far. In this way, you are able to stand in the centre of the equilibrated cross of the elements that is the mark of your grade. Remember that your position is as one who abides on the Threshold. As a Dominus Liminis, you shall be expected to prove your mastery at any time.

You shall construct and consecrate the magical Lamp, and in every way establish a fine and most subtle relationship with your Intuition.

A Dominus Liminis may at any moment withdraw from the association of the O∴ A∴ simply by notifying their appointed Guide in the Order.

I, _____ _____ [motto], do hereby resolve on this _____ day of _____ Anno _____ Sol in _____° of _____, that I shall direct the whole of my aspiration to the Glory of the Great Work, which is: To become *Illuminated* by my True Will.

May Horus crown the work, and bring me to his Knowledge and Conversation in due course!

Witness my hand:

Frater / Soror _____

O∴ A∴

OATH & TASK OF AN ADEPTUS MINOR 5° = 6□

Let the Adeptus Minor attain to the Knowledge and Conversation of the Holy Guardian Angel.

I, _____

[motto], do hereby resolve on this _____ day of

_____ Anno _____ Sol in _____° of _____, that I

shall do the Great Work, which is: To attain the Knowledge and

Conversation of the Holy Guardian Angel.

And may I be admitted to the Sanctuary of the Red Rose and Gold Cross right soon!

Witness my hand:

Frater / Soror _____

Curriculum of the Golden Dawn

Probationer 0° = 0□

A Probationer is any person of 21 years or more that has agreed to perform a spiritual exercise for one year on a strict daily basis, keeping a Record of their work. The *mudra* of the Probationer is that of *Horus the Enterer* and *Silence*. The Probationer is as one that waits on the Threshold; if their application is accepted they may then pass to the First Degree by signing the Oath of a Neophyte.

Neophyte 1° = 10□

A Neophyte is an Initiate of the O∴ A∴ in the First Degree. The grade corresponds to Malkuth of the Tree and the element of Earth. The *mudra* of the grade is that of *Baphomet*. The work at the level of the Neophyte becomes complex; design and construction of the Pentacle of Earth is a requirement, and its ritual consecration—instruction is given at the ceremony of their Initiation. The general techniques of magick are practised and some degree of mastery obtained. Tarot divination is studied and practiced. Qabalah and Gematria is studied and practiced. Contact is made with the angelic and elemental Spirits of Earth. The path of the Tav (path 32, *The Universe XXI*) must be negotiated; study and practice of the Enochian system is commenced, and the practice of Travelling and of Skrying in the Spirit Vision to the 30th Aethyr is undertaken.

General Methods

Rituals of the Pentagram and Hexagram; *asana* and *pranayama*.

1. Study and Practice of *Liber CMXXX*.

2. Design and Consecration of the Pentacle of Earth.

3. Greater Ritual of the Pentagram of Earth.

4. Assumption of the Egyptian Godform of Earth and Malkuth.

5. The Enterer of the Threshold for the 1° = 10□.

6. Hermetic Tantra-yoga: The Star and Snake.

7. Rising on the Planes to obtain a vision of the Spirits of Earth.

8. Pathworking: Path 32 *Tav*.

9. Skrying in the Spirit Vision to TEX, the 30th Aethyr.

41

Zelator 2° = 9□

A Zelator is any member of the O∴ A∴ in the Second Degree. The grade corresponds to Yesod of the Tree of Life and the element of Air. The *mudra* is that of *Ishtar*. The work involves a more concentrated approach to Hermetic Tantra-yoga. The *zeal* of the Zelator—the ascending Fire Snake—is aroused; the Zelator must pour their energised enthusiasm into the Great Work. Practical work focuses on perfection of *asana, pranayama* and *dharana*. The design and construction of the Dagger of Air is undertaken, and its ritual consecration by the Z Formula of the O∴ A∴ Contact is made with the angelic and elemental Spirits of Air. The paths to be mastered are those of *The Aeon XX* and *The Sun XIX* of Tarot (paths 31 Fire or Spirit, and 30 the Sun, respectively). Skrying and Travelling in the Spirit Vision to the 29th and 28th Aethyrs.

General Methods

Rituals of the Pentagram and Hexagram; *asana* and *pranayama* (Hermetic Tantra-yoga); development of *dharana*, the power of concentration.

1. The Ceremony for Making the Khu Perfect.

2. Design and Consecration of the Dagger of Air.

3. Greater Ritual of the Pentagram of Air.

4. Assumption of the Egyptian Godform of Air and Yesod.

5. The Enterer of the Threshold for the 2° = 9□.

6. Hermetic Tantra-yoga: The Lord of the South.

7. Rising on the Planes to obtain a vision of the Spirits of Air.

8. Pathworking: Path 31 *Shin* and Path 30 *Resh*.

9. Skrying in the Spirit Vision to RII and BAG, the 29th and 28th Aethyrs.

In addition to the above, exercises may be chosen from Sigil Magick, the Magical Ring, the Magical Memory or Tattwas and Swaras.

Practicus 3° = 8□

A Practicus is any member of the O∴ A∴ in the Third Degree. The grade corresponds to Hod of the Tree of Life and the element of Water. The *mudra* is that of *Isis of the Moon and Stars*. The work of the Practicus is focused towards control of the mind and consciousness expansion. The magical Cup is designed, constructed and consecrated. Tarot divination is continued. The Sepher Sephiroth is extended through the ongoing practical experimentation of the aspirant; the Practicus is expected to demonstrate expertise in Gematria and the Qabalah in general. Contact with the angelic and elemental Spirits of Water is made. The paths to be mastered are those imaged forth by *The Moon XVIII* (path 29 Pisces), *The Emperor IV* (path 28 Aries) and *The Tower XVI* (path 27 Mars). Skrying and Travelling in the Spirit Vision to the 27th and 26th Aethyrs is accomplished.

General Methods

Rituals of the Pentagram and Hexagram; *asana* and *pranayama* (Hermetic Tantra-yoga); the development of the mental powers including the expansion of consciousness and full use of the intellectual capacity.

1. Design and Consecration of the Water Cup.

2. Greater Invoking Ritual of the Pentagram of Water.

3. Assumption of the Egyptian Godform of Water and Hod.

4. The Enterer of the Threshold for the 3° = 8□.

5. Hermetic Tantra-yoga: The Lord of the South.

6. Rising on the Planes to obtain a vision of the Spirits of Water.

7. Pathworking: Path 29 *Qoph*, Path 28 *Tzaddi* and Path 27 *Pé*.

8. Skrying in the Spirit Vision to the 27th and 26th Aethyrs, ZAA and DES.

Philosophus 4° = 7▫

A Philosophus is any member of the O∴ A∴ in the Fourth Degree. The grade corresponds to Netzach of the Tree of Life and the element of Fire. The *mudra* of the grade is that of *Typhon*. The magical Wand is designed, constructed and consecrated. Contact is made with the angelic and elemental Spirits of Fire. The Philosophus should attain a level of proficiency in Astral Travelling and Skrying in the Spirit Vision, and must explore the 25th Aethyr. There is a focus in this grade on the selfless devotion characterised by *Bhakti Yoga*. Intellectual conceit, egotism, and spiritual vanity are among the dangers of the path.

General Methods

Rituals of the Pentagram and Hexagram; *asana* and *pranayama* (Hermetic Tantra-yoga); development of the Intuition; uniting the self with deity.

1. Devotion to Deity (Bhakti Yoga).

2. Design and Consecration of the Wand of Fire.

3. Greater Ritual of the Pentagram of Fire.

4. Assumption of the Egyptian Godform of Fire and Netzach.

5. The Enterer of the Threshold for the 4° = 7▫.

6. Hermetic Tantra-yoga: The Lord of the South.

7. Rising on the Planes to obtain a vision of the Spirits of Fire.

8. Skrying in the Spirit Vision to UTI, the 25th Aethyr.

In addition to the above, the Philosophus should make profound reflections on the Path.

[Completes the grades of the Golden Dawn. The next grade is that of the Dominus Liminis, who becomes a Probationer to the 2nd Order.]

The Temple in the Grades of the G. D.

1. Neophyte 1° = 10□

An arrangement for the Temple of Malkuth:

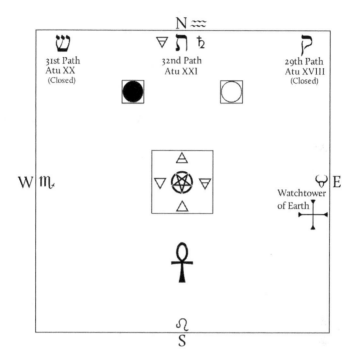

The consecration of the pentacle of Earth, a symbol of the Universe, means that the Neophyte acts as the Initiator of an elemental creature. In so doing, the Initiation of the Neophyte is made complete. The Z Formula is identical to that of Initiation, into any grade whatsoever. The inertia of the body and the material plane must be overcome to make progress with Rising on the Planes and to obtain a degree of mastery of the 32nd Path of Tav.

It is only by the way of the Tav on the middle pillar that the Neophyte can be admitted to the next grade, of Zelator. The pillars are therefore shown here in the North as the gateway to the Initiation of the 32nd Path.

2. Zelator 2° = 9□

An arrangement for the Temple of Yesod:

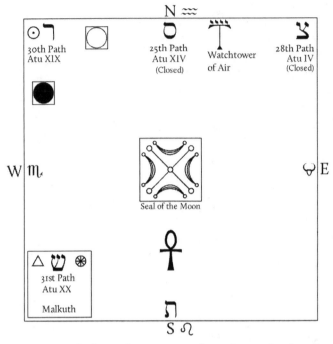

The Ceremony of the Khu or Passing through the Duat is a symbolic progression from Malkuth to Yesod. The consecration of the dagger of Air ceremonially confirms the aspirant in the elemental grade of Zelator. The work of the Zelator involves increased concentration in yoga and meditation. The rising Serpent Power, combined with ardent aspiration, produces a fiery *zeal* or fervour. Having gained a certain degree of mastery of the Astral Plane, the Zelator must use zeal in collecting and organising the necessary information and knowledge. The Seal of the Moon from the Kamea of the Moon is depicted on the central altar, to show the planetary nature of Yesod.

The pillars are shown before the 30th Path in this illustration, as though the Temple were arranged for the progression to the next grade. The fiery 31st Path must also be negotiated before admission is won to the grade of a Practicus. The 31st Path must be worked from Malkuth, so it is shown here enclosed by a square.

3. Practicus 3° = 8□

An arrangement for the Temple of Hod:

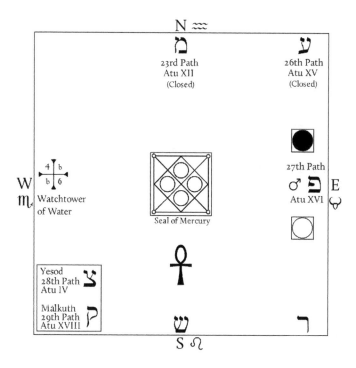

The Practicus affirms their admission to the Temple of Hod by consecrating their elemental cup for Water. Hod is the sphere of concrete mentation, and so the need for mental concentration is increased, while at the same time the consciousness must be expanded through the practice of yoga. Technical aspects of the work come to the fore, such as Qabalah and Gematria, and the perfection of the knowledge and use of the magical correspondences.

The Temple of Hod is shown here as arranged for the entry to the next grade of Philosophus, via the intense energy of the 27th Path. The 29th Path and the 28th Path must be worked from Malkuth and Yesod, so they are shown enclosed by a square.

4. Philosophus 4° = 7▢

An arrangement for the Temple of Netzach:

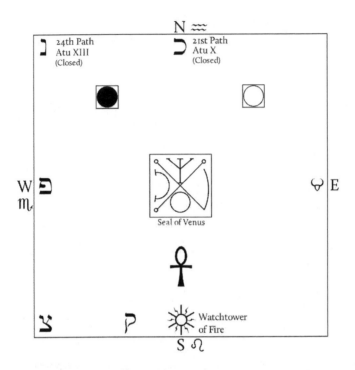

The Philosophus affirms their admission to the Temple of Netzach by ceremonially consecrating the wand for Fire. The move to the base of the right-hand pillar of the Tree is an unbalanced position, and so the Philosophus must overcome the powerfully seductive and delusional nature of the path of Venus by selfless devotion to deity—a seven month operation of Bhakti Yoga. Unlike other rituals and methods hitherto done, the Bhakti Yoga must be brought directly into the sphere of the person's everyday life. The paths of Atu XIII, *Death*, Atu XIV, *Art*, and Atu X *Fortune*, are closed to the Philosophus. Their glamour may nonetheless wield a powerful influence on the aspirant, which must be rigorously rejected. As the title of the grade suggests, the Initiate of this path is expected to produce their own insights into the Great Work.

5. Dominus Liminis

An arrangement for the Grade of the Portal:

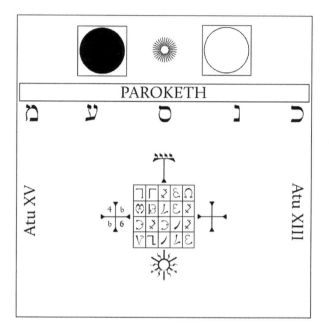

This shows the Temple arranged to represent the junction of the 25th Path and the 27th Path, on the darker side of the Veil of the Sanctum Sanctorum. The lamp of Spirit is nonetheless perceived as glowing faintly from the other side of Paroketh, and at the admission into the grade, a glimpse is gained. The Dominus Liminus acquires intellectual knowledge of the paths of *The Devil XV* and *Death XII*, but their knowledge is not fully open to him or her. The Dominus Liminis can only gain entry to the Order of the Rose Cross and the grade of Adeptus Minor by firm adherence to the middle pillar and, therefore, the 25th Path. In this time of a second Probationership—in which the heart of the aspirant will be weighed and tested further by the Lords of Initiation—the Dominus Liminis must equilibrate their self on the cross of four elements. This is symbolised by the four Watchtowers and the Tablet of Spirit that binds them all together.

The Song of the Stele

The *Song of the Stele* should be memorised. Make the *mudra* of offering oneself to the God, as shown in the depiction of Ankh af-na-khonsu on the *Stele of Revealing*. Recite the verses from the Egyptian Book of the Law, III: 37–38:

I am the Lord of Thebes, and I
The inspired forth-speaker of Mentu;
For me unveils the veilèd sky,
The self-slain Ankh-af-na-khonsu
Whose words are truth. I invoke, I greet
Thy presence, O Ra-Hoor-Khuit!

[Assume the first *mudra* of a Dominus Liminis, the Egyptian Ba:]

Unity uttermost showed!
I adore the might of Thy breath,
Supreme and terrible God,
Who makest the gods and death
To tremble before Thee:—
I, I adore thee!

Appear on the throne of Ra!
Open the ways of the Khu!
Lighten the ways of the Ka!
The ways of the Khabs run through
To stir me or still me!
Aum! let it fill me!

[Assume the *mudra* of the Pharaoh in the House of Gold. See Ra, Tum, Khephra and Ahathoor in the East, West, North and South:]

The light is mine; its rays consume
Me: I have made a secret door
Into the House of Ra and Tum,
Of Khephra and of Ahathoor.
I am thy Theban, O Mentu,
The prophet Ankh-af-na-khonsu!

[When saying "Bes-na-Maut", make the *mudra* of the Avenging Horus, beating the breast once for each syllable. When saying, "wise Ta-Nech", assume the *mudra* of the Pharaoh in the House of Gold. Assume the *mudra* of the Lord of the Stars when saying "Show thy star-splendour". After the last line, "Ra-Hoor-Khuit", make the *mudra* of Horus the Enterer followed by Silence:]

By Bes-na-Maut my breast I beat;

By wise Ta-Nech I weave my spell.

Show thy star-splendour, O Nuit!

Bid me within thine House to dwell,

O wingèd snake of light Hadit!

Abide with me, Ra-Hoor-Khuit!